A Smart Kid's Guide to
Playing Online Games

David J. Jakubiak

PowerKiDS
press
New York

For Cady and Kelly

Published in 2010 by The Rosen Publishing Group, Inc.
29 East 21st Street, New York, NY 10010

First Edition

Editor: Amelie von Zumbusch
Book Design: Julio Gil
Photo Researcher: Jessica Gerweck

Photo Credits: Cover © www.iStockphoto.com/Scott Dunlap; p. 5 © www.iStockphoto.com/Gene Chutka; p. 6 © Ansgar Photography/zefa/Corbis; p. 9 © Randy Faris/Corbis; p. 10 © Begsteiger/age fotostock; pp. 13 (left), 14, 21 Shutterstock.com; p. 13 (right) © www.iStockphoto.com/Quavondo Nguyen; p. 17 © Jim Craigmyle/Corbis; p. 18 © Heide Benser/Corbis.

Library of Congress Cataloging-in-Publication Data

Jakubiak, David J.
  A smart kid's guide to playing online games / David J. Jakubiak. — 1st ed.
    p. cm. — (Kids online)
  Includes index.
  ISBN 978-1-4042-8115-8 (library binding) — ISBN 978-1-4358-3350-0 (pbk.) — ISBN 978-1-4358-3351-7 (6-pack)
  1. Computer games—Juvenile literature. 2. Video games—Juvenile literature. 3. Computers and children—Juvenile literature. I. Title.
  GV1469.15.J35 2010
  794.8—dc22
                                    2009002615

Manufactured in the United States of America

Contents

Click to Play

Have you ever played an online game? Online games are games that you play through an **Internet connection** on a computer or a **mobile device**. Some online games are simple games that help teach math and reading skills. Other online games let you dress up cartoons or hit home runs into a roaring crowd. There are even games that let you make up characters to play in an online world.

There are some online games that you play by yourself. There are also lots of fun games that you can play with a friend across town or across the country on your **video-game console**.

Kids can pick from a huge number of online games.
There are games for kids who are interested in many subjects, such as sports,
cars, wild animals, cool clothes, TV shows, and math.

One of the great things about online games is that you can play them at night, when it is too late to visit friends or play outside.

Why Play?

Online games give **gamers** many reasons to play. These games can be changed often so that they never get boring. You can play them alone or with friends. Since they are played inside, online games can be played no matter how cold, rainy, snowy, or dark it is outdoors.

Playing online games can also help players learn skills they will use for the rest of their lives. For example, in the game Neopets, players take care of online pets. This is good practice for taking care of a living pet. Online games also teach players how important practice and planning are to winning.

Simple Games

There are many online games you can play just by visiting a Web site. These games use tools in your **Internet browser** to play sounds and **graphics**. You should not need to set up an **account** to play these games. If a game asks you to sign in, ask an adult before entering any facts about yourself.

Simple games can be found all over the Internet. Many are on the Web sites of zoos, **museums**, TV shows, and magazines. Others are on sites made just for games. For example, www.funbrain.com is one of these sites. It has several simple games that teach reading and math skills.

You can use a mouse or touchpad to play many simple online games. Other simple games use the arrow keys and space bar on your keyboard.

There are lots of sports games, such as this tennis game, that you can play on a game system that is connected to the Internet.

Kickoff Across Town

Imagine playing a football game and kicking off to your friend across town or playing Viva Piñata with a cousin in another state! A game system, such as an Xbox or PlayStation, can also be used to play games online. Video-game consoles use Internet connections to tie into a **network** for these games. An adult must sign up for you to become part of a system's network.

Once online, you can **download** games and videos. You can even set up your own character. Remember to be careful, though. These games are online, so you cannot always be sure with whom you are playing.

MMOGs

Some online games have thousands of players who all play together at the same time. These games are called massively multiplayer online games, or MMOGs. They are many people's favorite kind of game because they allow you to make characters, called avatars, to chat with other players and to play simple games in which you get more and more strength.

Two popular MMOGs are the Walt Disney Company's games Toontown and Club Penguin. In Toontown, players make cartoons that work together to fight bad guys. Club Penguin players make penguin characters, which they use to play games, make friends, and even pick pets, called puffles.

If you and your friends create characters in
the same MMOG, you can meet up online. This lets you have fun
with friends even if you live in different places!

Show the games you play online to an important adult in your life. This will both let the adult make sure that the games are safe and give you a chance to show off your online gaming skills!

Sign Up Safe, Play Safe

Some online games require players to become members of a Web site. Before signing up for any site, talk to a trusted adult, such as a parent or a guardian. Show the adult the site and the game you want to play. Carefully read the rules of the site together. Remember, not all sites are safe and many are not meant for kids.

If you do sign up, you should pick a **screen name** that hides your real name. Never pick a screen name that is close to your real name or one that will give away your e-mail address. Do not use the name of your school, camp, or sports team as part of your screen name, either.

Griefers and Worse

Online games are fun. However, there are some mean players who can make playing online anything but fun. For example, griefers are gamers who bully. They play to mess up a game, break rules, and make trouble for other players.

Other players use games to try to meet people in real life. These players may ask to see a picture of you or want to know your age, real name, or password. They may even pretend to be someone you know. This is not allowed. Never share personal facts with another player. Never visit someone you met online in person. Keep online games on the computer!

If other gamers make you feel scared, hurt, or unsafe, remember that they are the ones who did something wrong. Do not blame yourself!

It is important to talk to a trusted adult if other gamers are bothering you online. Together, you can decide how to deal with the gamers who are troubling you.

Ending Problems

Facing a griefer or rule breaker can make you feel angry or hurt. However, do not strike back alone. Show an adult what has happened. Report the problem to the site's **moderator**.

Most games offer ways players can help keep griefers away. For example, Club Penguin players who have been playing the game for 30 days can become "secret agents," who help keep the game safe.

Do not blame yourself for the way griefers act and never feel bad for taking steps to stop them. Remember that reporting griefers will keep them from picking on other people, too!

Take a Break

When you play an online game, you can get really into it. Reaching another level can seem all-important. Getting points can seem like the only thing that matters. You may even put off doing homework, getting a snack, or taking your dog for a walk.

If this happens, take a break. Try to spend only 2 hours in front of a TV or computer screen each day. Instead of playing online games, get some fresh air. Try playing basketball with your friends, walking your dog, or visiting a park. If you cannot go outside, you can still draw, paint, read, listen to music, or play a board game. Online games are lots of fun, but they will still be there tomorrow!

Even if you really like online games, remember to make time to play outside. One way to make sure you spend time outdoors is to become a member of a sports team.

Safety Tips

- Only visit sites that you know are safe. Searching for games can take you to unsafe sites.

- Never download anything before asking an adult.

- Go online with friends you know in person, so that you will have people with whom you can safely play online.

- When you are playing online games, remember to take breaks.

- Never use your name or age as part of your screen name.

- Write reviews of games and share them with your friends.

- Have a family video-game night to show your games to the adults in your family.

- If you play games in which you talk online, use a tool called voice-masking software to hide your real voice.

Glossary

account (uh-KOWNT) A membership to a Web site.

download (DOWN-lohd) To add files from a Web site to a computer.

gamers (GAY-merz) People who play online or video games.

graphics (GRA-fiks) Pictures and artwork that are shown on a screen.

Internet browser (IN-ter-net BROW-zer) Something that lets people use their computers to see Web sites.

Internet connection (IN-ter-net kuh-NEK-shun) Something that connects a computer to the Internet.

mobile device (MOH-bul dih-VYS) A small computer people can carry around.

moderator (MO-deh-ray-tur) Someone who makes sure that people get along.

museums (myoo-ZEE-umz) Places where art or historical pieces are safely kept for people to see and to study.

network (NET-wurk) A group of connected computers.

screen name (SKREEN NAYM) A name someone uses online.

video-game console (VIH-dee-oh-gaym KON-sohl) A tool that lets people play video games.

Index

Web Sites

Due to the changing nature of Internet links, PowerKids Press has developed an online list of Web sites related to the subject of this book. This site is updated regularly. Please use this link to access the list:
www.powerkidslinks.com/onlin/games/